CONTENTS

EGYPT

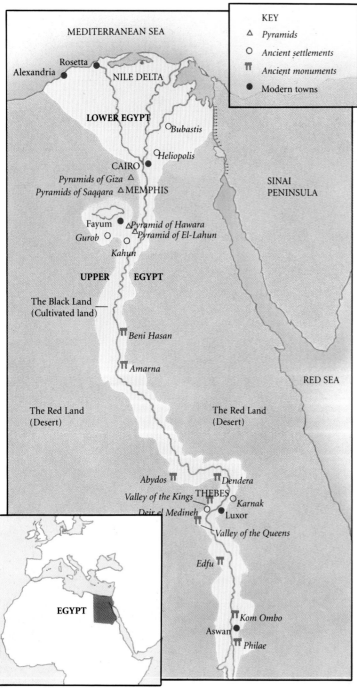

KEY
△ Pyramids
○ Ancient settlements
Ⅱ Ancient monuments
● Modern towns

MEDITERRANEAN SEA

Alexandria
Rosetta
NILE DELTA

LOWER EGYPT

○Bubastis

○Heliopolis

CAIRO
Pyramids of Giza △
Pyramids of Saqqara △MEMPHIS

SINAI
PENINSULA

Fayum △Pyramid of Hawara
Gurob ○ ○ △Pyramid of El-Lahun
Kahun

UPPER EGYPT

The Black Land
(Cultivated land)

Ⅱ Beni Hasan

Ⅱ Amarna

RED SEA

The Red Land
(Desert)

The Red Land
(Desert)

Abydos Ⅱ Ⅱ Dendera
Valley of the Kings THEBES
Deir el Medineh ○ Ⅱ○ Karnak
Ⅱ Luxor
Valley of the Queens

Edfu Ⅱ

Ⅱ Kom Ombo
Aswan ●
Ⅱ Philae

EGYPT

For thousands of years the people of Egypt have depended on the River Nile. Most of their country is desert. It is too hot and dry to grow crops or raise animals there. But along the river there is a strip of rich green land. This is good for farming.

The first Egyptians

People first came to live beside the Nile over 200,000 years ago. They hunted the birds and animals that lived in the swamps. As the centuries passed they learned to grow crops. Every year the River Nile flooded and spread mud over their land. This helped their crops to grow.

They produced so much food that some of the people did not need to be farmers. They learnt new skills. They built the great pyramids that you can still see along the River Nile today. We call the people who built the pyramids, the Ancient Egyptians.

◀ This map shows the ancient ruins and some of the modern towns along the River Nile in Egypt.

▲ This is a picture of the Nile at Beni Hasan. You can see where the narrow green strip of farmland meets the dry desert.

Archaeologists have learned a lot about the Ancient Egyptians from the ruins of their pyramids and temples. Beautiful paintings on the walls of the tombs give us clues about their everyday lives.

This photograph shows two knives and some arrowheads. Egyptian hunters made these from flint. They are at least 6,000 years old. ▶

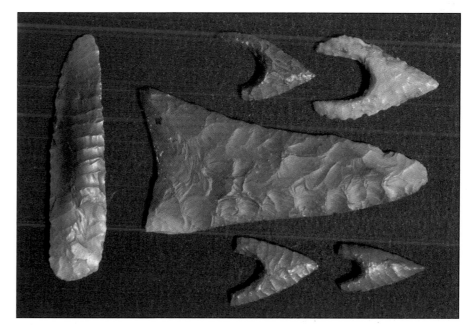

The people of Ancient Egypt

The most important person in Ancient Egypt was the king. After about 1450 BC he was called the 'pharaoh' instead of the 'king'. The people closest to the pharaoh were the wealthy noblemen. They advised him and made sure his wishes were carried out.

Priests

The Ancient Egyptians worshipped many gods and goddesses. They believed that if the gods became angry the River Nile would not flood each year. Their green fields would become dusty desert. Their crops and animals would die, and eventually they would die too. A priest's job was to keep the gods happy by offering gifts to them. Priests were very important people in Ancient Egypt.

Scribes and craftsmen

The next most important people in Egypt were the scribes. Other people respected them because they could read and write. After them came the craftsmen – such as builders, painters, sculptors, carpenters and potters.

▲ This is a painting from a tomb, made in about 1250 BC. It shows a priest wearing a leopard skin.

Farmers

In some ways farm workers were the least important people. They were not respected like priests or scribes. But everyone depended on the farmers to grow enough food for all the people.

This tomb painting shows a nobleman hunting in the marshes. It was made in about 1430 BC. ▼

FAMILIES

Many tomb paintings and statues from Ancient Egypt show families. You can see some of them on these pages. The Ancient Egyptians thought families were very important. Even their gods and goddesses were grouped into small families.

▲ This small statue shows a dwarf called Seneb with his family. Seneb was in charge of the royal family's clothes.

◄ This painting is from the tomb of a man called Ankherkhau. It shows him with his wife (on the left) and his young daughters.

Men

Men were treated as more important than women in Ancient Egypt. Farmers passed down their farmland to their sons. Craftsmen taught their sons how to do their jobs, so the sons could take over from them when they died.

Beside this family there is a table piled with offerings of food for the gods. ▼

When a man grew old his family respected him even more. He remained in charge of the family until he died, even if he had young, strong sons or grandsons who could take over from him.

Marriage

Girls got married from about the age of 11. Their husbands were usually quite a lot older. They did not have a wedding in the way we do today. The parents of the bride and groom just agreed that the couple should marry. Then the bride left her father's house and went to her new home. A crowd of people followed her in a procession.

This vase is in the shape of a mother holding a child. ▶

This wooden model shows women weaving. It was found in a tomb and it is over 4,000 years old. ▼

Husbands were expected to treat their wives well, as this writing tells us:

"Love your wife with all your heart.
Fill her belly, clothe her back,
Soothe her body with ointment.
Make her happy as long as you live."

A woman was allowed to keep anything she owned when she got married – she did not have to hand it over to her husband. If her husband died, she was allowed to keep a share of his property too. It was quite easy to get divorced. The wife went back to live with her parents and then she could marry someone else if she wanted to.

This vase was probably used to store make-up. It is in the shape of a woman playing a lute. ▶

Passing on the family blood

In Ancient Egypt a man became king by marrying the queen. This is because it was women who passed on the family blood. If the king and queen had a son and a daughter, the royal blood passed to the daughter. Their son could become king by marrying their daughter. All families passed on their family blood from mother to daughter, but in ordinary families it was unusual for brothers and sisters to marry.

These are statues of the princess Nofret and her husband. She is wearing a jewelled headband and a collar made of beads. ▼

Children

Having babies was dangerous, and mothers often died. The Ancient Egyptians had great respect for women who were able to produce many children. Poor families needed lots of children to help them with their work. They needed children to look after them when they grew old, too.

Children are often shown in tomb paintings. One way to spot them is by their hair. Both girls and boys had a lock of hair hanging down on one side of their heads. It is called the 'sidelock of youth'.

▲ This carved picture is from the throne of the pharaoh Tutankhamun. It shows him being looked after by his wife.

The sun is shown in this carving. It means that the sun god is protecting the pharaoh Akhenaten and his family. ▶

Clothes

Egypt is a hot, dry country, so people did not need many clothes. Often, children wore no clothes at all. Men wore short kilts. When it got cooler in the evenings they put on warm cloaks.

▲ This young prince (left) is wearing fine linen clothes. He has the sidelock of youth, held back with a jewelled clip.

Women draped and folded big pieces of linen around themselves to make their dresses. Some of the fashions were very elegant. Linen is a cloth that is cool to wear in hot weather, so it was used by the rich and by the poor.

Poor people wore rough, plain linen. Very fine linen was used to make clothes for rich people such as nobles and scribes. Sometimes their clothes were coloured with bright natural dyes. Archaeologists have found wooden chests full of clothes in Egyptian tombs.

The writing on the top of this chest of clothes says that it belonged to a sea captain called Daneg-Ro.▼

Education

Most children did not learn to read and write. Boys learned how to do the same jobs as their fathers. Mothers taught girls how to run the home.

People who could read and write were called scribes. The Ancient Egyptians respected their skills. A man called Dua-Khety told his son, Pety, that every other job had something wrong with it. He said that a soldier might get killed, weaving was woman's work, and a potter was always covered in earth. To be successful, Pety needed to become a scribe.

▲ A small statue of a scribe hard at work.

This painting was made in around 1250 BC. It shows a royal scribe (on the right) playing a board game called senet. ▶

16

Games and parties

The Egyptians did not spend all their time working. Children enjoyed playing together. They had a few toys, such as rag dolls and balls.

Children from wealthy families sometimes went to parties with their parents. They are shown on tomb paintings of parties, standing behind their mother's or father's chair.

▲ These women are enjoying a party. One of them (second from the right) is playing a flute.

AT HOME

▲ This painting shows an Egyptian house. The windows are very high up, to try to keep the rooms cool.

The Egyptians used mud to build their homes. They shaped it into bricks and left the bricks to dry and harden in the hot sun.

Most houses had one big room that opened on to the street. There was a smaller room behind this. Some houses had stairs leading to the roof. People slept up there in very hot weather.

Food and cooking

Most Ancient Egyptian families did not eat much meat. Sometimes they ate small animals they had caught in the desert, or birds they had trapped beside the river. They ate a lot of raw vegetables and flat, round bread. They used ovens made of clay to cook food. These were often outdoors – it was too hot to cook inside.

People such as scribes and priests had better food. The priests were especially well fed. This was because they were allowed to eat the gifts of meat that people brought to the temples. These gifts were offerings for the gods.

▲ This is a woman grinding corn. She is breaking up the grains by rubbing them over a flat stone slab.

This wooden model was found in a tomb. It shows fishermen at work. You can see some fish in the net between the two boats. ▶

19

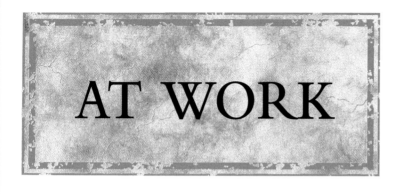

AT WORK

Craftsmen and builders

Imhotep was King Zoser's chief architect. About 2670 BC, he built the Step Pyramid at Saqqara for the king. We think this was the first stone building in the world. Later, Ancient Egyptians worshipped Imhotep as the god of architecture.

Some tomb paintings and models show craftsmen at work. This model shows carpenters sawing and shaping wood. ▶

We do not know the names of many other Ancient Egyptian builders and craftsmen. But we can tell how skilled they were by looking at their work. You can see some of their paintings and carved statues in this book. They also made beautiful furniture, glass and jewellery.

In this model, the men are blowing through thin pipes to make a fire extremely hot. They heated special sand in the fire and made it into glass. ▶

Farmers

Farm work was very hard. Farmers and their families worked in the fields from sunrise to sunset. They had a break in the middle of the day, when it was too hot to work.

This painting shows a man ploughing. Two oxen pull the plough. His wife walks behind him, scattering the corn seed. ▼

There were a few months every year when farmers could not work in the fields. The land was covered by the flood water from the Nile. Farmers did other work at this time. When pyramids were being built, the farmers helped with that work during the flood months.

▲ A man and his wife harvesting wheat.

This tomb painting shows farmers making their cattle walk over stalks of wheat. They did this to separate the grains from the stalks. It is called threshing. ▶

22

When the floods were over, each farmer marked out the edge of his fields. Then he was ready to start ploughing. His wife or the older children walked behind the plough, scattering the seed.

These men are winnowing. ▼

Harvest time was hard work for the whole family. The farmer cut the wheat with a sharp, curved knife. His wife picked up the fallen wheat. Then it was threshed and winnowed to separate the wheat grains from the stalks.

The family had to give some of their grain to the pharaoh as a tax. The rest was ground into flour and used to make bread.

TOWNS AND VILLAGES

The stone temples and pyramids of Ancient Egypt took many years to build. The men who worked on them needed somewhere to live, so villages and towns grew up around the building sites. Later, great cities grew up near the temples. The capital city was called Memphis.

▲ The workers' village at Deir el-Medineh.

◀ The ruins of a royal palace. The parts that have survived are made of stone.

Archaeologists do not know very much about Ancient Egyptian towns. They have spent most of their time excavating the tombs and temples.

▲ This is the palace of the pharaoh Akhenaten. Some of the mud-brick walls have survived here. They are over 3,000 years old.

Houses – and even the royal palaces – were built of mud brick. Not many of these have survived. One village that has been excavated is at Deir el-Medineh. The men who dug and decorated the royal tombs in the Valley of the Kings lived here. Archaeologists have found out a lot about family life from this village. They have even found letters – and people's complaints about their neighbours!

GODS AND FESTIVALS

This bronze statue shows Isis feeding her son Horus. ▼

The Ancient Egyptians worshipped many gods and goddesses. They believed that a god or goddess looked after each part of their lives. For example, a god called Bes looked after women and children. He was also the god of music and merriment.

The gods and goddesses were grouped into families. The most important family of gods was Osiris, the god of the dead, his wife Isis, and their son Horus.

▲ This funny-looking god is Bes.

A different god or goddess was worshipped in each of the great temples. Ordinary people never went inside the temples. Only the priests and the pharaoh were allowed into these holy places.

▲ Egyptian temples all had a sacred lake where the priests sailed the god's ship. This one is inside the temple of Amun-Re at Karnak.

Ordinary people did take part in religious festivals. A festival called Opet was held in honour of the chief god, Amun-Re. The priests carried a statue of the god from his temple at Karnak to another one at Luxor. People had a day off work to watch the procession. They asked for the god's help as his statue passed by.

THE NEXT WORLD

The Ancient Egyptians believed that when a person died, he or she went on a long journey to another world. They put food and drink for the journey into the grave. The graves of poor people were just holes in the desert sand. Wealthy people had tombs cut out of rock. The pyramids were built as tombs for some of the pharaohs.

▲ This is the body of an Ancient Egyptian who died more than 6,000 years ago.

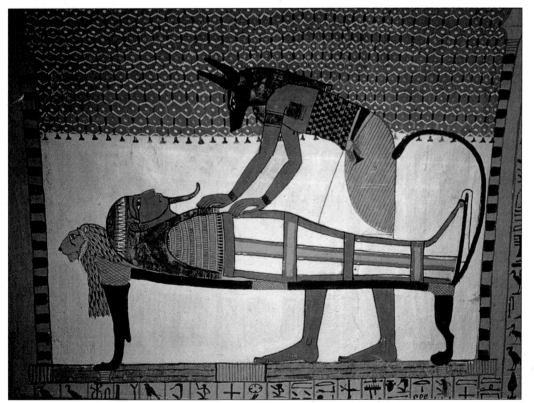

◄ This painting shows a god called Anubis. He is preparing a body for its journey to the next world.

The bodies of wealthy people were mummified. This means that their bodies were treated so that they would not decay. All their most precious belongings were put into the tomb with them, so that they could use them in the next world. When archaeologists opened the tomb of the boy king Tutankhamun they found piles of jewellery, fine clothes and furniture.

▲ This painting shows a dead person's heart being weighed in a balance against the Feather of Truth. This was part of the test to see if a person could enter heaven.

The Ancient Egyptians believed that after they died they would have to take a test. This test was to find out if they had led a good life. If they passed the test the god of the dead, Osiris, would welcome them into heaven. They believed that they would live happily for ever in heaven, with all the family members who had died before them.

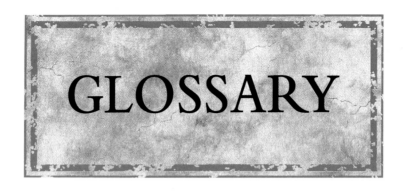

GLOSSARY

Archaeologists People who try to find out about the past by studying the remains of buildings and objects such as pottery or bones. Usually the remains are buried underground, so archaeologists have to dig to find them.

Architect A person who decides what a building should look like and makes a drawing for the builders to work from.

BC This means 'Before Christ'. The year Jesus Christ was born is counted as the year 0. Years before this date are counted backwards, so 10 BC is ten years before Christ was born, and 1450 BC is 200 years further back in time than 1250 BC.

Centuries One century is 100 years.

Dyes Chemicals that are used to colour cloth. In Egyptian times they were made from natural products such as plant juices.

Excavating Digging very carefully to uncover buried buildings.

Flint A type of stone.

Kilts Skirts worn by men.

Linen A cloth made from a plant called flax. It is a bit like cotton.

Offerings Gifts of food or other goods that people made to the gods and goddesses.

Pyramids Huge buildings with four sloping, triangular sides. In Ancient Egypt they were built as tombs for the royal family.

Sacred Holy; something that belongs to a god or goddess.

Temples Buildings where offerings were made to the gods and goddesses.

Threshed Beaten to separate the grain from the stalks.

Tombs The places where people's bodies were left after they died. A tomb might be a hole cut out of rock, or a room inside a pyramid.

Weaving Linking threads together to make cloth.

Winnowing Throwing grain up into the air to remove any bits of stalk left in it after it has been threshed. The grain falls back to the ground but the stalks, which are lighter, blow away in the breeze.

Books to read

Clothes of the Ancient World by Christine Hatt (Belitha, 2000)
Look Inside an Egyptian Tomb by Brian Moses (Hodder Wayland, 1999)
The Nile Files (series) by Philip Wooderson (Watts, 2000)
Pharaohs and Embalmers and other jobs for Ancient Egyptians by Anita Ganeri (Heinemann Library, 1997)
The Secret Diary of Prince Tutankhamun by Philip Ardagh (Watts, 1998)
Women in Ancient Egypt by Fiona Macdonald (Belitha 1999)

Places to visit

Ashmolean Museum, Beaumont Street, Oxford OX1 2PH.
A very good collection that tells you about everyday life in Egypt.

British Museum, Great Russell Street, London WC1B 3DG.
The largest and finest collection of all kinds of Egyptian objects in Britain.

Fitzwilliam Museum, Trumpington Street, Cambridge CB2 1RB.
Many ancient Egyptian works of art.

Manchester Museum, Oxford Road, Manchester M13 9PL.
Several newly displayed Egyptian galleries.

Petrie Museum, University College London, Malet Place, London WC1.
A collection of objects of everyday Egyptian life.

If you visit Egypt on holiday there is a splendid Ancient Egyptian collection in the Cairo Museum. Many European countries, like the ones listed below, also have excellent collections.

France: Paris (Louvre Museum).

Germany: Berlin (Ägyptisches Museum); Munich (Staatlichen Sammlung Ägyptischer Kunst Museum).

Holland: Leiden (National Museum).

Italy: Florence (Archaeological Museum); Rome (Vatican Museums);

Turin (Archaeological Museum).

INDEX